THE POWER OF COMPOUNDING

Build Strong Routines, Develop Good Habits, Inspire Growth, and Improve Self-Worth to Build Wealth.

PRADIP DAS

© **Copyright 2024 - All rights reserved.**

The content contained within this book may not be reproduced, duplicated, or transmitted without direct written permission from the author or the publisher. Under no circumstances will any blame or legal responsibility be held against the publisher, or author, for any damages, reparation, or monetary loss due to the information contained within this book. Either directly or indirectly.

Legal Notice:

This book is copyright protected. This book is only for personal use. You cannot amend, distribute, sell, use, quote or paraphrase any part, or the content within this book, without the consent of the author or publisher.

Disclaimer Notice:

Please note the information contained within this document is for educational and entertainment purposes only. All effort has been executed to present accurate, up to date, and reliable, complete information. No warranties of any kind are declared or implied. Readers acknowledge that the author is not engaging in the rendering of legal, financial, medical or professional advice. The content within this book has been derived from various sources. Please consult a licensed professional before attempting any techniques outlined in this book.

By reading this document, the reader agrees that under no circumstances is the author responsible for any losses, direct or indirect, which are incurred as a result of the use of information contained within this document, including, but not limited to, — errors, omissions, or inaccuracies.

Author Profile

Table of Contents

Table of Contents 4

Introduction 5

Compounding for Financial Freedom 13

Compounding Success in Career 23

Compounding in Personal Development 32

Building Strong Relationships through Compounding 41

The Impact of Compounding on Happiness 50

Family and Legacy 61

Compounding Small Steps for Big Health Outcomes 71

Compounding for Community and World Impact 79

Spiritual Growth Through Compounding 86

Compounding in Self-Discipline and Habit-Building 94

Compounding Impact on the Environment 105

Challenges to Compounding and How to Overcome Them 115

The Journey vs. The Destination 122

Conclusion 128

Introduction

When people hear the word "compounding," most think of investments and interest rates. However, compounding is much more than a financial concept. It's a powerful force that can affect every area of our lives. Simply put, compounding is the process where small, steady actions build on each other over time, leading to outcomes far greater than their parts. When we understand compounding, we start to see how little efforts, repeated consistently, can create remarkable changes in our lives. This is not just about getting rich; it's about getting better, bit by bit, in anything we choose.

What is Compounding? More Than Just Money

Compounding is often linked to money because it's easy to see the effects of compounding in a savings account or investment. With money, we deposit a sum and earn interest on it, and then, over time, we also earn interest on the interest. The value grows, not just by adding, but by multiplying. But imagine applying this same idea to our skills, habits, and choices in life.

Every small choice or effort we make has the potential to grow into something bigger. A single page read today leads to a full book in a month. A five-minute walk every day can lead to a healthier body over time. Every small kindness shown to others can strengthen relationships. Just as a tiny spark can lead to a fire, the little things we do each day can build up and create a powerful change in our lives.

The Compound Effect on Our Life Choices

Life is shaped by the choices we make, and compounding shows us how even the smallest choices can add up. Imagine two people - one who eats a little healthier every day and another who has a daily sugary snack. After a day or even a week, the difference between these two people may not seem obvious. But over months and years, one is likely to be in better health, while the other might struggle with health issues. The small daily choice, repeated over time, leads to very different outcomes. This is the compounding effect in our daily decisions.

We see this effect in personal growth as well. Someone who practices a skill, such as playing an instrument or learning a language, for just 10 minutes each day will likely become quite skilled over time. Another person who practices irregularly or not at all will find it difficult to reach the same level. The compound effect of practice and consistency shows up in every area of life, from learning to relationships, and from career growth to personal habits.

Why Small Actions Matter Over Time

One of the most interesting things about compounding is how small actions can lead to big results. In the beginning, our efforts may feel small and unimportant. The results can seem invisible, and we may feel tempted to give up. But the power of compounding lies in patience. When we stick with small actions over time, they build on each other. Each step, no matter how small, gets us closer to our goals. This slow and steady growth often leads to success in ways that quick bursts of effort cannot.

In the beginning, a tree is just a small sapling, delicate and easily overlooked. But over time, with consistent sunlight, water, and nutrients, it becomes a strong tree. This growth doesn't happen overnight. It's slow, steady, and the result of small, consistent actions working together. In the same way, our lives are shaped by the small, steady efforts we make every day. It's not just the big changes that matter; it's the tiny, consistent steps that truly transform our lives.

Compounding as a Life Skill

Learning how compounding works can be one of the most valuable skills we gain. It teaches us the value of patience and the importance of long-term thinking. In a world that often praises quick results and instant gratification, understanding the power of compounding gives us a different perspective. We start to see the value in starting small and growing gradually, rather than rushing for quick outcomes.

Compounding is not just a tool for building wealth; it's a mindset for building a meaningful life. By taking small, positive actions each day, we can improve our skills, relationships, and even our sense of happiness. It encourages us to focus on what we can do today, however small it might be, and trust that these efforts will grow over time.

The Journey Begins

The journey of compounding is one that takes time, but the rewards are well worth it. Whether it's improving your health, building a skill, or saving for the future, small actions repeated consistently will add up to a life of growth and fulfillment. This book will help you to understand what compounding is, and how it can become a guiding force in your life. We'll look at stories, examples, and practical steps you can take to bring the power of compounding into your daily routine. With this knowledge, you can begin your journey towards steady improvement and meaningful change. Every big achievement starts with a small step, and every great life is built on the small, positive actions we choose each day.

Compounding for Financial Freedom

Compounding is a simple yet powerful concept that can change how we look at money. At its core, compounding is the process where money grows over time by earning returns on both the original amount and the interest it has already made. Imagine a snowball rolling down a hill. As it rolls, it picks up more snow and gets bigger. Compounding works in a similar way with money. As your investments grow, they start earning on both the money you put in and the gains they've made along the way.

In financial terms, if you invest a certain amount of money, over time, not only will that amount grow, but the growth itself will start to grow. This leads to faster and larger returns as time goes on. This is the core idea of compounding, and it's the reason why many successful investors say, "Time in the market is more important than timing the market." The earlier you start, the more your wealth can grow.

How Investing Early Multiplies Wealth

Starting early gives compounding more time to work. To understand this better, let's take the example of two friends, Sara and Rahul. Both decide to invest in their 20s, but Sara starts at 25 and invests $5,000 every year until she's 35, then stops adding more money but leaves her investments to grow. Rahul waits until he's 35 to start, then invests $5,000 every year until he's 60. Surprisingly, even though Rahul put in money for 25 years and Sara only invested for 10 years, Sara still ends up with more money by the time they both reach 60. This is the power of starting early.

When we start investing early, our money has more time to grow, and even small investments can turn into a large sum over time. Warren Buffett, one of the world's wealthiest people, is a great example. He started investing when he was only 11 years old, and today, much of his wealth has come from letting his money grow over decades. His story teaches us that starting early can make a huge difference in building wealth.

For young people just beginning to invest, even small amounts can have a big impact over time. Let's say you put away just $100 every month into an investment that grows by 7% each year. By the end of 30 years, you could end up with around $120,000, and most of that would be the growth of the original $36,000 you put in. Compounding makes this possible by adding the gains back into the original amount and allowing them to grow together.

One of the best ways to understand compounding is to look at the real-life stories of people who have used it to achieve financial freedom. Warren Buffett's journey, as mentioned before, is an incredible example. He began with a small investment when he was young, but by consistently investing and allowing his wealth to grow over time, he accumulated one of the largest fortunes in the world.

Another real-life example is the story of Ronald Read, a janitor and gas station attendant who amassed nearly $8 million by the time he passed away in his 90s. Read didn't earn a high income, but he was careful with his money and invested regularly in stocks. By buying shares in well-known companies and holding onto them for decades, he allowed compounding to work in his favor. His story shows that you don't have to be wealthy to benefit from compounding; it's accessible to anyone who is willing to invest consistently over time.

These stories show that patience is key when it comes to compounding. The people who built great wealth didn't do it by making quick money or taking high risks. Instead, they took a steady approach, allowing their investments to grow gradually over the years.

Building a Legacy with Compound Wealth

One of the most exciting parts of compounding is its potential to create lasting wealth, not only for yourself but for future generations. When we think about building wealth, it's common to focus on reaching a comfortable retirement or achieving financial independence. However, compounding can go beyond that and help build a legacy. By letting your investments grow long enough, you can create wealth that lasts even after you're gone, benefiting your children, grandchildren, and beyond.

Imagine a family that starts a small investment fund for their child when they are born. By the time the child reaches adulthood, even a modest yearly contribution can turn into a significant sum. If they continue to let the investment grow, they can build a family fund that supports education, healthcare, or other important needs for generations.

For example, some families create scholarship funds, start charities, or support community programs with their compounded wealth. This type of giving back not only helps those in need but also builds a sense of pride and purpose for the family members involved. Compounding doesn't just grow wealth; it can create a long-lasting positive impact.

Warren Buffett, in his later years, committed a large part of his wealth to philanthropy. His donations to charity have already made a huge impact, and his decision to give most of his wealth to causes he cares about will continue to benefit people for years to come. Buffett's example shows how compounding can help build a legacy that makes a difference in the world.

Making Compounding Work for You

To make compounding work for you, there are a few important things to keep in mind. First, it's essential to start as early as possible. The earlier you start, the more time your money has to grow. If you haven't started yet, don't worry; it's never too late. The best time to start is now.

Second, consistency is key. Try to invest a set amount regularly, even if it's small. Regular contributions help to grow your investments steadily over time. It's also important to avoid taking out money too early, as this can interrupt the compounding process and slow down your wealth-building.

Finally, choosing the right type of investments matters. Stocks, mutual funds, and index funds often offer higher returns over time, which can speed up the compounding effect. However, it's important to choose investments that match your financial goals and risk tolerance.

In short, compounding is a powerful tool that can help anyone build wealth, achieve financial independence, and even create a lasting legacy. By starting early, investing consistently, and allowing your investments to grow over time, you can make the most of the compounding effect. You don't have to be wealthy to benefit from compounding. With patience and a steady approach, compounding can turn small investments into significant wealth over time. The journey may be long, but the rewards can be life-changing, providing both financial security and the opportunity to make a positive impact for years to come.

Compounding Success in Career

When we think about success in our careers, it's easy to imagine big leaps—like getting a promotion or landing a dream job. However, most success comes from small, consistent steps. This idea is known as incremental growth. Just like saving a little money every month can lead to a large sum over time, improving your skills and knowledge bit by bit can lead to big changes in your career.

Maya Angelou, a celebrated poet and civil rights activist, faced many struggles, including a challenging childhood before she became famous for her writing. Yet, she was determined to improve her skills. Angelou worked various jobs while honing her craft as a writer. Each poem she wrote and each story she told added to her knowledge and experience. Over time, her dedication and incremental growth helped her become one of the most influential voices in literature.

To experience similar growth, start by setting small goals. Instead of aiming to be an expert overnight, focus on learning something new every week. This could be reading articles, taking online courses, or attending workshops. As you accumulate knowledge, you will notice that you become more confident in your abilities, which will open up new opportunities in your career.

Networking Over Time

Another essential aspect of career success is networking. Building strong connections takes time, but these relationships can have a significant impact on your career. Networking isn't just about collecting business cards; it's about forming genuine relationships with people in your field.

Consider the example of Sheryl Sandberg, the former COO of Facebook and author of *Lean In*. Sandberg has always emphasized the importance of building relationships throughout her career. Early on, she made connections at Google that later helped her when she joined Facebook. She understood that networking is not only about getting ahead but also about supporting others along the way. Her ability to connect with people and maintain those relationships played a crucial role in her success.

To build your network, attend industry events, join professional organizations, and engage in online communities. Remember that networking is not just about what others can do for you; it's also about how you can support them. Offer your help when possible, whether it's sharing knowledge, providing introductions, or simply being a supportive friend. As you invest in these relationships over time, you'll create a network that can help you grow in your career.

How to Leverage Compounding in Career Advancement

To leverage compounding in your career, think about how your skills, connections, and experiences can build on one another. Each new skill you learn can open doors to new opportunities. Each connection you make can lead to collaborations and job offers.

Consider the example of Satya Nadella, the CEO of Microsoft. Nadella began his career at Microsoft as a young engineer. He continuously sought to learn and grow within the company. Over the years, he took on various roles that allowed him to develop a diverse skill set in technology and leadership. His commitment to learning and his ability to connect different areas of expertise ultimately led him to become the CEO, where he transformed Microsoft into a more innovative and agile company.

To apply this in your career, identify how your skills can complement each other. If you're good at writing and marketing, for instance, consider how these skills can work together to promote a project. Look for ways to learn from different fields and find intersections where you can excel. This approach can create a powerful advantage in your career, as you develop a unique skill set that sets you apart from others.

The Ripple Effect of Consistency and Hard Work

Consistency and hard work are the foundation of compounding success in your career. Just as a small investment can grow into a large sum over time, consistent effort in your work can lead to impressive results.

Think about the journey of Serena Williams, a world-renowned tennis player. From a young age, she committed to practicing regularly and improving her game. She faced numerous challenges, including injuries and fierce competition, but her dedication to training and hard work helped her achieve greatness.

Each practice session added to her skills, and her consistent effort led her to win numerous championships and set records in the sport.

To apply this lesson, commit to working hard in your career. Set a daily routine that allows you to focus on your goals. This could mean dedicating time each day to improving your skills, networking, or working on projects. Stay committed to your tasks, even when the progress feels slow. Over time, you will see the results of your hard work compound, leading to significant advancements in your career.

Putting It All Together

As you journey through your career, remember that success doesn't happen overnight. It requires patience, consistent effort, and a willingness to learn and connect with others.

1. **Focus on Incremental Growth**: Set small goals for skill development and knowledge acquisition. Celebrate your progress, no matter how small.
2. **Build Your Network**: Make genuine connections with others in your field. Offer support and seek mentorship, knowing that these relationships will pay off over time.
3. **Leverage Your Skills**: Identify how your different skills can work together. Find unique intersections that make you stand out in your industry.
4. **Commit to Consistency**: Stay dedicated to your goals. Even when progress feels slow, remember that

hard work will lead to compounding success.

By understanding and applying these principles, you can create a career path that leads to lasting success. Your efforts will compound over time, and you will find yourself reaching new heights you once thought were out of reach. Stay focused, keep learning, and nurture your connections. The future is bright when you commit to a life of growth and giving.

Compounding in Personal Development

Compounding doesn't just apply to money or investments. It plays a big role in personal development, too. When you work on yourself a little each day, you begin to build habits and skills that grow over time. Just like saving a bit of money every month, small improvements in your learning, habits, and mental strength can add up to huge results in the long run. In this chapter, we'll explore how continuous learning and small, consistent habits can lead to meaningful growth. We'll also discuss how mental strength and resilience grow over time, using a famous athlete as an example of personal development success.

The Power of Continuous Learning and Self-Improvement

Learning doesn't stop when we finish school. In fact, some of the most important lessons in life happen outside the classroom. Continuous learning means always looking for ways to gain new skills, understand the world better, and improve yourself. Just like putting small amounts into a savings account, each bit of learning adds to your personal "wealth." Over time, these little gains build upon each other.

Imagine learning something new every day. It doesn't have to be a huge thing—it could be a new word, a life lesson from someone else, or a skill like cooking or budgeting. When you learn consistently, you become more adaptable and better at solving problems. This kind of growth makes life feel richer and fuller because you're always moving forward. With time, you'll look back and realize how much you've grown just by staying curious and open to new ideas.

How Habits, Even Small Ones, Transform Over Time

Habits are the small actions we do every day that shape who we become. They might seem small at first, like reading a few pages each night, exercising for a few minutes, or taking a moment each day to reflect on your goals. But over time, these small habits grow into something powerful. They become part of your daily routine, and with each repetition, they make you a little better.

Let's take reading, for example. If you read for just 15 minutes every day, you might not feel any different at first. But after a month, you've read for over seven hours. After a year, that small habit has added up to nearly 90 hours of reading. Think about how much knowledge and perspective you could gain with that much time spent learning! This is the power of small habits. Over time, they become part of who you are, helping you grow and become more skilled in ways that might surprise you.

A famous example of the power of small habits is found in NBA player Michael Jordan. Jordan didn't just become one of basketball's greatest players overnight. He committed to daily practice, even when he didn't feel motivated. His routine included not only intense physical training but also mental exercises and visualization techniques. By sticking to these habits day after day, Jordan compounded his skills and mental strength, eventually becoming a basketball legend. His story shows us how small, consistent habits, practiced over time, can lead to incredible results.

Compounding Mental Strength and Resilience

Mental strength and resilience are key parts of personal development, and like anything else, they grow over time. When we talk about resilience, we're talking about the ability to bounce back from challenges, stay strong under pressure, and keep going even when things get tough. Building mental strength doesn't happen all at once. It happens little by little, as you face small challenges, learn from them, and keep moving forward.

Each time you overcome a setback, you become a bit stronger and more confident in your ability to handle the next challenge. Over time, this resilience compounds, just like savings in a bank. The more you practice handling tough situations, the better you get at facing whatever life throws your way.

A strong example of this can be seen in the journey of tennis star Rafael Nadal. Nadal faced numerous injuries throughout his career, from wrist injuries to knee issues. However, each time he came back stronger, using his past experiences to fuel his determination. His mental strength and resilience allowed him to keep pushing forward, eventually winning numerous Grand Slam titles. His story shows us how resilience, compounded over time, can help overcome even the most challenging situations.

Real-Life Examples of Personal Development Success

Real-life examples show us that personal growth is a journey, not a quick fix. Many successful people have reached their goals by focusing on continuous self-improvement, forming strong habits, and building mental resilience over time.

One inspiring example is the life of inventor and businessman Thomas Edison. Edison's path to success wasn't smooth—he faced thousands of failed experiments before finally inventing the light bulb. But Edison kept working every day, experimenting and learning from his mistakes. His persistence paid off, and his inventions changed the world. Edison's story teaches us that even when things are difficult, small, consistent steps forward can lead to big achievements.

Another example is Steve Jobs, co-founder of Apple. Jobs didn't begin with a large company or vast resources. He started small, learning about technology and design bit by bit. Over time, his skills and vision grew, and he developed a series of products that transformed the tech industry. Jobs' journey shows us the impact of compounding in personal growth. Each year, he added to his understanding and skill set, which eventually helped him lead one of the most innovative companies in the world.

In the end, compounding in personal development is about being patient and consistent. Small efforts, whether they're habits, learning, or building mental strength, add up over time. Just as financial investments grow with regular contributions, our personal growth increases with each small effort we make. Even tiny steps forward make a difference. When you look back, you'll be amazed at how far those small steps have taken you. This is the power of compounding in personal development—it's not about doing everything at once, but about making steady progress every day.

Building Strong Relationships through Compounding

Compounding works wonders in relationships too. When we invest small acts of kindness, trust, and patience into our friendships and family bonds, the benefits grow over time, leading to stronger, more meaningful connections. Relationships built on these small but consistent actions create a deep foundation that can endure challenges and make good times even better.

The Accumulation of Small Acts of Kindness and Attention

Building a solid relationship doesn't happen overnight. Small gestures—a warm smile, a kind word, remembering birthdays, or lending a listening ear—accumulate over time. Each small act may seem minor on its own, but together, they become powerful. Just like saving small amounts can build into a large sum in a bank, small acts of kindness build a reservoir of warmth and trust in our relationships.

Mother Teresa became beloved worldwide not because of one grand act but because of thousands of small, consistent acts of kindness. She spent years caring for those who were neglected and forgotten, and her legacy of love and compassion continues to inspire people around the world. In our own lives, we can apply this idea by being kind and attentive to those around us. These small acts, done often, create bonds that grow stronger with each gesture, even if they seem small in the moment.

How Compounding Trust Builds Lasting Connections

Trust is a cornerstone of any strong relationship. It doesn't just appear; it's built gradually, over time. Trust grows with each promise kept, each time we're there for someone, and each moment of honesty. When we're reliable in both small and big ways, it sends a clear message that others can depend on us.

For example, Mahatma Gandhi built trust with his followers through years of unwavering dedication to his principles and people. His honesty, kindness, and commitment gained him not only followers but deep loyalty. This trust didn't develop from one speech or action; it grew through his consistent actions over time. In our everyday lives, we can apply this idea by keeping our word, being there when it matters, and being honest with others. Each act of reliability adds up, creating a strong bond of trust that only grows over time.

Emotional Bank Accounts in Friendships and Family

In relationships, we can think of an "emotional bank account" where each kind act, supportive word, or thoughtful gesture is like a deposit. Every time we're rude, insensitive, or hurtful, we make a withdrawal. To keep relationships strong, we need to ensure we're making more deposits than withdrawals. This "account" isn't about keeping score; it's about recognizing the importance of consistent kindness and support over time.

Imagine you have a friend who always checks in on you when you're feeling down and remembers the small details you share with them. Every time they do this, they're adding to the emotional bank account. When, on the other hand, they accidentally forget an important event or cancel plans, it might feel like a small withdrawal. However, if they've made enough positive deposits, the relationship stays strong because of that built-up balance of positive interactions. By regularly "depositing" kindness, support, and understanding, we build up our relationships so that they can handle occasional mistakes or conflicts.

The Role of Compounding in Forgiveness and Reconciliation

In every relationship, misunderstandings, mistakes, and conflicts are bound to happen. When they do, forgiveness becomes essential for healing and growth. Forgiveness can be challenging, especially when someone has caused us pain. However, when we choose to forgive, we make a positive "deposit" in our relationship, showing that we value it more than the hurt caused by a mistake.

Forgiveness is a bit like clearing away a roadblock. It allows us to keep moving forward without carrying the weight of resentment. Over time, choosing to forgive can compound into a stronger, healthier relationship. This doesn't mean forgetting or accepting harmful behavior; it means letting go of the negative emotions that keep us stuck. Each act of forgiveness adds to the strength of the relationship, helping it grow and withstand future challenges.

One inspiring example of forgiveness is Nelson Mandela. After being imprisoned for 27 years, Mandela chose to forgive his captors and worked toward peace and unity in South Africa. His decision to forgive was not only a single act but a series of choices that led to a stronger, more unified country. Mandela's forgiveness wasn't just about one moment; it was a lifetime of commitment to reconciliation, showing how the compounding effect of forgiveness can bring healing on a grand scale.

In our personal relationships, forgiveness works in a similar way. By choosing to forgive small wrongs and misunderstandings, we create space for love, understanding, and growth. Over time, this pattern of forgiveness builds a strong bond that can handle bigger challenges, because both people know they are valued beyond their mistakes.

Finally, the concept of compounding reminds us that relationships need regular care and attention. Small acts of kindness, steady trust, and a willingness to forgive are the building blocks of strong connections. These little actions, repeated over time, strengthen our friendships and family bonds, helping them grow deeper and more resilient.

By understanding and applying the power of compounding in our relationships, we can create connections that last a lifetime. Each small gesture, act of trust, or moment of forgiveness adds up, making our relationships strong enough to stand the test of time. In this way, the power of compounding isn't just a financial principle—it's a way to enrich our lives and the lives of those we care about.

The Impact of Compounding on Happiness

Just like compounding grows wealth over time, simple daily habits can compound to create a lasting sense of happiness. Small actions, repeated daily, can lead to big changes in our overall joy and contentment. These actions don't need to be grand gestures. They can be simple routines like taking a few minutes each morning to breathe deeply, enjoying a cup of tea, going for a short walk, or calling a friend. These small moments allow us to slow down and appreciate what we have.

One key practice that helps with compounding happiness is gratitude. Taking a moment each day to recognize things we are thankful for can be very powerful. Writing down one or two things in a notebook or even saying them out loud can help shift our focus from what's missing in life to what we already have. Over time, this habit can create a deeper sense of contentment and satisfaction.

Another daily practice is kindness. When we do small acts of kindness, like helping a neighbor or listening to a friend, we feel good, and that happiness grows. These actions don't just help others; they help us feel more connected and fulfilled. Even simple acts of kindness, done consistently, can make a lasting impact on our happiness.

How Positive Mindsets and Gratitude Compound Over Time

Our mindset plays a huge role in how happy we feel over time. A positive outlook doesn't mean ignoring challenges or pretending everything is perfect. It means choosing to see the good in situations, learning from setbacks, and trusting that things can improve. Over time, this way of thinking can become a habit, allowing us to approach life with more calmness and confidence.

Gratitude, in particular, compounds as it becomes part of our daily routine. When we make a habit of appreciating the good things, we start noticing more of them. Over weeks, months, and years, this practice can shift how we see the world. Challenges might still come, but we're better prepared to handle them because our minds are more focused on the positives. A grateful attitude changes how we respond to life, making us happier overall.

Real-Life Stories of Happiness Achieved Through Consistency

Consistent daily habits have helped many people find lasting happiness. One inspiring story is from the life of the Dalai Lama. He practices compassion, gratitude, and meditation daily. These routines have helped him stay calm and joyful even in difficult times. Despite losing his homeland and facing many hardships, the Dalai Lama's commitment to these habits has kept him peaceful and happy. He shares that simple acts of kindness and a focus on gratitude have been his greatest sources of joy. This shows us that consistency in positive habits can lead to deep and lasting happiness, regardless of life's challenges.

Another example is J.K. Rowling, the author of the *Harry Potter* series. Rowling faced many struggles before her success, including financial troubles and personal losses. Despite these hardships, she found happiness through small daily practices, like writing. Writing was her way to express herself, and over time, it helped her build confidence and a sense of purpose. This daily habit eventually brought her happiness and success. This reminds us that even during tough times, staying consistent with positive practices can help us feel happier and fulfilled.

Practical Tips to Develop a Compounded Happiness Mindset

Creating a happiness mindset that compounds over time involves adding small, positive practices into daily life. Here are some simple ways to start:

1. **Start a Gratitude Routine**: Each day, write down one thing you are grateful for. This can be as simple as enjoying a meal, a moment with family, or a good laugh. This practice helps shift your focus from what's missing to what's present in your life, building a foundation for joy over time.
2. **Engage in Small Acts of Kindness**: Do something kind every day, even if it's small. This could be giving someone a compliment, offering help, or just

listening to someone who needs it. Kindness creates a feeling of connection and adds to your sense of happiness.

3. **Set Aside "Quiet Time" Daily**: Take a few minutes each day to be alone with your thoughts. This could be through meditation, breathing exercises, or simply sitting quietly. This practice helps calm the mind and makes it easier to handle stress, leading to a happier outlook.

4. **Practice Mindfulness**: Try to be fully present in whatever you are doing. When eating, take the time to enjoy each bite. When talking to someone, listen carefully without thinking about what you'll say next. Being mindful

allows you to appreciate the moment, adding to your daily happiness.

5. **Focus on Self-Improvement**: Dedicate a few minutes each day to learning something new. This could be reading, practicing a skill, or setting a small personal goal. The feeling of progress, even if it's small, adds to a sense of accomplishment and happiness over time.

6. **Surround Yourself with Positive Influences**: Spend time with people who lift you up and avoid those who drain your energy. Positive relationships contribute to a lasting sense of happiness. Connecting with positive people can have a compounding effect on how happy you feel.

7. **Celebrate Small Wins**: Life is full of little successes. Each time you accomplish something, whether it's completing a task or reaching a goal, take a moment to celebrate. Recognizing small wins keeps you motivated and builds a foundation for long-term happiness.
8. **Reflect Regularly**: At the end of each week, take a few minutes to reflect on what went well. Thinking about positive moments can help you appreciate them even more and prepare you for a new week with a positive outlook.

A Life of Compounded Happiness

Compounded happiness doesn't happen overnight; it builds gradually through small, steady actions. The key is consistency. By committing to small daily habits like gratitude, kindness, and mindfulness, we set the stage for a happier life. Just as money grows with time through compounding, so does happiness. When we invest in these positive actions every day, they add up, creating a more joyful life that lasts.

Building a happiness mindset isn't about being cheerful all the time. It's about creating a strong foundation that helps us handle both good times and hard times. With each act of kindness, each moment of gratitude, and each step toward growth, we become a little happier. Over time, this happiness grows, not only making our own lives better but also spreading to those around us.

In the journey of life, small steps can create big changes. By focusing on positive habits that compound over time, we're not just creating moments of joy—we're building a life filled with it. Through gratitude, kindness, and a positive mindset, we can make happiness something that grows steadily, giving us a sense of purpose and fulfillment that lasts.

Family and Legacy

Family is where we first learn about values, kindness, respect, and patience. Just like financial compounding, values and principles grow stronger when passed down through generations. In this chapter, we'll explore how teaching values to the next generation, spending meaningful time together, and focusing on what truly matters can help create a lasting family legacy. Let's look at how we can use the power of compounding to make our family bonds stronger and ensure that our values live on through the lives we touch.

Teaching Values and Principles to the Next Generation

Passing down values is a gradual process. We can teach important lessons through our daily actions, words, and choices. The values we show become examples for younger family members, who then grow up to reflect these principles in their own lives. This way, values get passed down, just like a baton in a relay race, and they continue to grow over time.

Mahatma Gandhi, one of the most respected leaders in history taught principles of truth, nonviolence, and compassion not only through his words but through his actions. His values inspired not just his children but an entire nation. Gandhi's lessons on kindness, truth, and respect are still alive in people's minds around the world. His example shows how powerful values can be when we live them fully and pass them on.

To instill values, families can focus on qualities like honesty, patience, and generosity.

Showing respect for others, regardless of their background or beliefs, can be a foundation for raising kind and empathetic individuals. Over time, these principles become part of a family's identity, shaping the next generation.

How Family Rituals and Time Create Bonds

Spending quality time together as a family is one of the strongest ways to build lasting connections. Simple, meaningful moments create memories that last for years and strengthen family ties. Family rituals, even small ones, help create a sense of togetherness and continuity. Whether it's a weekly dinner, celebrating birthdays, or taking regular family trips, these shared moments deepen family bonds.

John D. Rockefeller, one of the wealthiest people in history, understood the importance of family values and unity. He established family meetings and set up gatherings that allowed his family to connect regularly. This tradition has carried on, helping family members stay close and aligned in their values. The Rockefeller family not only passed down wealth but also values of hard work, unity, and respect. Through these family gatherings, each generation has been able to grow with a shared sense of identity and purpose.

The key here is not how big or elaborate the ritual is but rather the consistency. Simple traditions become deeply meaningful when they're done regularly. This regular time together strengthens the bonds between family members, allowing values to be shared naturally, creating lasting connections.

The Role of Compounding in Parenting and Mentorship

Just like financial compounding, the principles we pass down grow stronger over time when they're nurtured. Parenting and mentorship are two ways we help others grow, shaping the values of the next generation. When parents teach their children values and skills from an early age, they're planting seeds that will continue to grow as their children mature.

A good example of compounding in mentorship is the story of Helen Keller and her teacher, Anne Sullivan. Helen Keller was deaf and blind, and her early life was filled with challenges. But with Anne Sullivan's patience, support, and dedication, Keller learned to communicate, read, and write. Over time, Keller grew into a powerful advocate for people with disabilities. Anne Sullivan's guidance had a ripple effect, helping Keller become a global inspiration. This example shows how mentorship, when given consistently, can help someone reach great heights.

In parenting, small lessons about kindness, responsibility, and honesty can be taught through daily actions and words. When parents practice patience, understanding, and hard work, their children absorb these values. The lessons may not seem significant at the moment, but over the years, they shape the character and values of the next generation. Each conversation, each example, adds to a foundation that continues to grow, just like compounding interest.

Leaving a Legacy Beyond Material Wealth

Leaving a legacy goes beyond passing down money or possessions. True legacy is about passing down values, stories, and lessons that will guide future generations. Wealth might last a few generations, but values and principles can live on forever, shaping the world in a positive way.

Mother Teresa left a legacy that went far beyond material wealth. Her life was filled with acts of compassion and service, helping those in need. Mother Teresa's legacy isn't measured by money; it's measured by the countless lives she touched through her kindness and care. Her values continue to inspire people worldwide, showing that true wealth comes from giving and making a difference.

For families, focusing on what matters most—kindness, honesty, integrity, and compassion—can create a legacy that lasts. While financial assets can support future generations, it is the values that give them purpose and guidance. Leaving behind a legacy of generosity, respect, and hard work provides a strong foundation for those who come after us.

Building a Lasting Family Legacy

A family legacy is something we build over time, through small, consistent actions. As we teach values, create meaningful family moments, and mentor the younger generation, we're helping to shape a legacy that grows over time. This is the power of compounding in family life: every kind word, every family ritual, and every lesson learned becomes part of something much larger.

We may not see the immediate effects, but with patience, these values will grow. Future generations will carry forward the principles we taught them, passing them down to their children and beyond. A family that values honesty, kindness, and perseverance creates a legacy that will stand strong, leaving a positive mark on the world for years to come.

In the end, the power of compounding values lies in the small choices we make each day. Just as compounding interest grows our wealth, compounding values build a lasting legacy. As we focus on kindness, integrity, and respect, we create a family culture that will benefit generations to come. This is the true legacy we can leave—a legacy that makes the world a better place, one small act at a time.

Compounding Small Steps for Big Health Outcomes

Let's say you decide to cut one sugary drink from your daily routine. Instead of a soda, you choose water or tea. This simple swap can save you about 150 calories a day. If you do this every day for a year, you could lose around 15 pounds just from this one change! Small changes in our diet and exercise can add up to huge improvements over time. That's the magic of compounding.

Now, think about exercise. If you start by walking just 10 minutes a day, you're making a positive choice for your health. Over time, as you feel stronger and more energized, you might find yourself walking 20 minutes, then 30. These small steps can lead to significant health benefits, such as better heart health, increased energy levels, and improved mood.

Building Mental Health Through Positive Daily Practices

Taking care of your mind is just as important as caring for your body. Daily habits can help build mental strength and resilience. Simple practices like gratitude, mindfulness, and even just taking a few deep breaths can make a big difference.

For example, the famous writer Maya Angelou often spoke about the importance of gratitude. Each day, she would write down things she was grateful for. This practice helped her stay positive and focused, even during tough times. By regularly reminding ourselves of the good in our lives, we can build a more positive mindset.

Another great practice is mindfulness. This means being present in the moment, without worrying about the past or future. Just a few minutes of mindful breathing each day can help reduce stress and improve your overall mental health.

The Connection Between Physical Health and Personal Success

When we think about success, we often picture achievements in our careers or personal lives. However, our physical health plays a huge role in this. If we feel good physically, we are more likely to perform better in all areas of our lives.

Tennis champion Serena Williams works hard to maintain her physical fitness. Her training not only keeps her in top shape for competitions, but it also boosts her confidence and mental sharpness. When she steps onto the court, she knows she has done everything possible to prepare herself. This level of readiness contributes to her success.

In many cases, people who prioritize their health tend to be more productive and creative. They can focus better and have the energy to tackle challenges. Making health a priority can lead to better results in work and personal projects.

Practical Steps for a Healthier, Compounded Lifestyle

Now that we understand the importance of small changes and the connection between health and success, let's look at some practical steps we can take to create a healthier lifestyle.

Start Small: Pick one or two areas to focus on. Maybe you want to eat more fruits and vegetables or increase your daily activity. Begin with small, achievable goals. For instance, if you want to eat more fruits, aim to add one piece of fruit to your daily diet.

1. **Make It a Habit**: Try to repeat your small changes regularly until they become habits. If you're walking for 10 minutes, do it at the same time each

day. Once it feels natural, you can gradually increase the time or intensity.

2. **Track Your Progress**: Keeping track of your changes can motivate you to stick with them. You can use a journal or a mobile app to note your daily meals, exercise, and how you feel. Seeing your progress can boost your confidence and encourage you to keep going.

3. **Connect with Others**: Share your goals with friends or family. You can support each other in making healthier choices. Joining a group or class can also provide encouragement and motivation.

4. **Celebrate Small Wins**: Recognize your achievements, no matter how small. If

you walked 10 extra minutes or chose a salad over fries, give yourself credit. Celebrating these wins can help keep you motivated to continue.

5. **Stay Flexible**: Life can get busy, and that's okay. If you miss a workout or indulge in a treat, don't be too hard on yourself. Focus on getting back on track. Remember, it's about the long-term journey, not perfection.
6. **Keep Learning**: Stay curious about health and wellness. Read books, listen to podcasts, or attend workshops. The more you learn, the more empowered you will feel to make positive changes in your life.

By taking these practical steps, you can gradually build a healthier lifestyle. The key is consistency. Over time, the small steps you take will lead to big changes in your health and well-being.

Here, we explored how small changes in diet and exercise can multiply over time, how daily practices can improve mental health, and how physical health connects to personal success. Just like saving money, small efforts in health can lead to significant rewards. With patience and commitment, you can create a healthier, more fulfilled life. The journey may take time, but the rewards are worth it.

Compounding for Community and World Impact

Every big change in the world often starts with small actions. Think about how a tiny seed grows into a massive tree. In the same way, when individuals take small steps to help others, these actions can lead to significant improvements in communities and beyond.

Mahatma Gandhi was a leader in India's fight for independence. Gandhi believed in the power of small, everyday actions. He encouraged people to spin their own cloth instead of buying it from British factories. This small act was about more than just cloth; it was a way for people to support their economy and stand up against oppression. His simple idea brought millions together and helped inspire a nation to seek freedom. This shows how small acts of service can add up to create significant social changes.

Compounding Knowledge and Skills to Create Social Impact

When we think about compounding, we often picture money growing in a bank account. However, compounding can also refer to knowledge and skills. When we learn something new, we can share that knowledge with others. As we teach, we often learn even more, creating a cycle of growth that benefits everyone involved.

When individuals come together to share their skills, they can solve problems that affect their communities. For instance, a group of people might learn about gardening and decide to create a community garden. As they share their skills and knowledge with others, more people join in, leading to a network of gardeners. This group can grow not just food, but also friendships and a sense of community. These connections can help reduce food insecurity and promote healthy eating, showing the power of compounding knowledge for a greater cause.

The Role of Compounding Efforts in Charity and Volunteer Work

Charity and volunteer work are powerful ways to create social change. When people come together to help those in need, their combined efforts can create a more significant impact than individual actions. Each volunteer may contribute a little time or resources, but when combined, these efforts can transform entire communities.

Mother Teresa dedicated her life to helping the poor and sick in India. What started as a small effort to care for the homeless grew into a global mission. Mother Teresa's simple acts of kindness inspired thousands of others to join her cause. Her work led to the establishment of numerous charities and organizations aimed at helping the less fortunate. By compounding her efforts with those of many others, she changed the lives of countless people, highlighting how collective actions can lead to significant social change.

When communities come together for a cause, they can amplify their efforts. For example, a local charity might hold a food drive. If a few people donate food, it helps, but if hundreds of people contribute, they can feed thousands. This compounding effect not only helps those in need but also strengthens community ties. People feel a sense of belonging and purpose when they work together, creating a cycle of goodwill and support.

There are many inspiring stories of communities that have been transformed by combined efforts. One such story comes from **Banjul**, the capital of The Gambia. For years, this community struggled with waste management, leading to health issues and pollution. A group of local residents decided to take action. They started a clean-up campaign, gathering their neighbors to pick up trash and educate others about waste disposal.

At first, the group was small, but as they spread the word, more people joined their efforts. Schools began to participate, and local businesses offered support. Over time, the community developed a culture of cleanliness and responsibility. Not only did this improve the environment, but it also brought people together, fostering a sense of pride in their community. This shows how compounded efforts can lead to a healthier and happier community.

Another powerful example is the **Ice Bucket Challenge**, which started as a simple challenge among friends to raise awareness for **ALS (Amyotrophic Lateral Sclerosis)**. What began as a few videos on social media quickly went viral, inspiring millions to pour ice water over their heads and donate to ALS research. This grassroots movement raised over $220 million for research and support, leading to breakthroughs in understanding the disease. The success of the Ice Bucket Challenge shows how small, fun actions can compound into massive global movements, bringing attention and resources to important causes.

In conclusion, compounding isn't just about money. It's about the power of small actions to create significant change in our communities and the world. Whether through knowledge sharing, volunteer work, or collective efforts, every individual has the potential to make a difference. When we come together to help one another, we create a ripple effect that can transform lives and communities for the better.

So, let's remember the power of our small actions. Every little bit counts, and together, we can make a big difference.

Spiritual Growth Through Compounding

Spiritual growth is like planting a seed in a garden. At first, you might not see much happening. But with patience and care, the seed grows into a beautiful plant. This chapter is about how small spiritual practices can lead to big changes over time, creating a sense of peace and fulfillment in our lives.

Think of spiritual practices as daily habits that can make us feel better inside. Just like exercising or eating healthy food, these practices help us grow emotionally and spiritually. When we make time for activities like meditation, prayer, or simple reflection, we are planting seeds of positivity and inner strength.

When you meditate, you take a few moments to quiet your mind and focus on your breath. This practice helps reduce stress and clears your mind. Over time, even just a few minutes a day can lead to a calmer and happier life. Many people find that when they meditate regularly, they feel more in tune with themselves and the world around them. It's a simple habit that can create a big change in how we feel.

Prayer is another powerful practice. It doesn't have to be complicated. It can be as simple as talking to a higher power, expressing gratitude, or asking for guidance. Over time, prayer can create a deep sense of connection and purpose. People who pray often say they feel supported and less alone in their struggles.

Reflection is about taking time to think about our experiences. This could be through journaling or simply sitting quietly and thinking about our day. By reflecting on our feelings and actions, we learn more about ourselves. This practice can help us understand what matters most in our lives, guiding us towards a more meaningful existence.

How Meditation, Prayer, and Reflection Add Up

These practices—meditation, prayer, and reflection—may seem small on their own, but together they create a powerful effect. When we consistently engage in these activities, they compound, much like interest in a savings account. Over time, the benefits grow, leading to deeper peace and understanding.

Mahatma Gandhi was known for his deep commitment to spiritual practices. Every day, Gandhi set aside time for prayer and meditation. These moments helped him find clarity and strength, especially during challenging times. Gandhi believed that spiritual growth was essential for personal and social change. Through his consistent practices, he not only found inner peace but also inspired millions around the world to seek nonviolent solutions to conflict.

Just like Gandhi, many people have found fulfillment through spiritual compounding. A woman named Tara started practicing gratitude every morning. She would write down three things she was thankful for before starting her day. At first, it felt like a small and simple task. However, over time, she noticed a shift in her perspective. Instead of focusing on what she lacked, Tara began to see the abundance in her life. This small practice helped her feel happier and more content, even during tough times.

Applying Spiritual Compounding for a Life of Meaning

To apply spiritual compounding in our lives, we can start small. Here are a few simple ways to begin:

1. **Set Aside Time Daily:** Choose a few minutes each day for meditation, prayer, or reflection. It doesn't have to be long—just a few moments can make a difference.
2. **Create a Gratitude Journal:** Write down things you are grateful for each

day. This can shift your focus and help you appreciate what you have.

3. **Practice Mindfulness:** Take a few moments throughout your day to pause and check in with yourself. Notice your feelings, your breath, and your surroundings. This practice can help you feel more connected to the present moment.
4. **Connect with Nature:** Spend time outdoors. Nature has a way of calming us and helping us feel grounded. A walk in the park or simply sitting in your garden can be a spiritual practice.
5. **Engage with Others:** Share your spiritual journey with friends or family. Talking about your experiences can deepen your understanding and create a sense of community.

These small steps can lead to significant changes in how we view ourselves and our lives. Just like any other area of life, spiritual growth is a journey. By committing to our practices, we can find a deeper sense of peace and fulfillment over time.

As we explore spiritual growth through compounding, let's remember that it's not about reaching a specific destination. It's about enjoying the journey and learning more about ourselves along the way. Each practice, no matter how small, contributes to our overall well-being.

In closing, spiritual growth is a gift we give ourselves. It opens the door to a life filled with meaning and connection. Like a garden that flourishes with care, our spirits can thrive through consistent, simple practices. By investing a little time each day, we can nurture our inner selves and find the peace we seek.

So, let's take that first step. Choose a practice that resonates with you and start today. The journey may be long, but each small effort adds up, leading us toward a richer, more fulfilling life.

Compounding in Self-Discipline and Habit-Building

Building strong habits takes time and effort, much like planting a seed and nurturing it to grow into a tree. It doesn't happen overnight; rather, it is a process of making small changes consistently over time. The first step is to identify the habits you want to develop. Start by choosing one or two simple habits that align with your goals. For instance, if you want to get fit, you might start with a daily ten-minute walk or drinking an extra glass of water each day.

Next, create a plan to incorporate these habits into your daily routine. Use a calendar or a journal to track your progress. When you see your achievements written down, it motivates you to keep going. It's important to be patient with yourself during this time. Sometimes, habits take longer to form, and that's okay. What matters is that you stay committed and keep making those small efforts.

As you get used to these new habits, you can gradually increase their complexity or duration. If your goal is to read more, start with just a page a day and slowly work your way up to a chapter or two. This method of gradual increase helps you build confidence and reinforces your ability to stick to the habit.

The Cumulative Effect of Discipline in All Aspects of Life

Discipline acts like a snowball rolling down a hill. At first, it might be small and unnoticeable, but as it rolls, it gathers more snow and grows larger. In the same way, practicing self-discipline in one area of life can lead to improvements in other areas.

For example, when you wake up early, you have more time to plan your day, exercise, or enjoy a peaceful breakfast. This extra time can help you feel more organized and less rushed. As a result, you may find yourself being more productive at work or in your personal projects.

Discipline in one habit can positively affect others. When you choose to exercise regularly, you often find yourself eating healthier and sleeping better. This ripple effect can lead to overall well-being and greater life satisfaction.

Thomas Edison, the inventor of the light bulb, worked tirelessly, often spending long hours in his workshop, driven by his goal of creating a working light bulb. His discipline in his work didn't just lead to the invention of the light bulb; it also opened the door to countless other innovations. Edison's consistent efforts in one area of his life significantly influenced many aspects of science and technology.

How Micro-Changes Lead to Major Habit Formation

Making tiny changes in your daily routine can lead to significant results over time. This idea is at the heart of building strong habits. Micro-changes are small adjustments that may seem insignificant on their own but can compound into something substantial when repeated regularly.

For example, if you want to improve your writing skills, instead of trying to write a novel right away, start by writing just one paragraph a day. This small action is easy to do and doesn't feel overwhelming. As you continue this practice, your writing will improve, and you might find yourself gradually increasing your output. Soon enough, what started as one paragraph a day can lead to pages and, eventually, a full book.

The key is consistency. When you stick to your micro-changes, they become part of your daily routine, and before you know it, they form a strong habit. This is the power of compounding. Small, consistent actions can lead to major transformations over time.

Another example of this principle can be seen in the life of Michelle Obama. As the First Lady of the United States, she focused on promoting healthy eating and fitness among children. She didn't aim for a complete overhaul of everyone's diet and exercise habits at once. Instead, she encouraged small changes, like adding more fruits and vegetables to meals or taking the stairs instead of the elevator. These micro-changes encouraged families to adopt healthier lifestyles over time, illustrating how small steps can lead to big impacts.

Success Stories of People Who Transformed Through Discipline

Many Indian celebrities have shown that discipline and steady habits can lead to remarkable achievements. Their journeys remind us that dedication to daily actions is often the real foundation of success.

One powerful example is Amitabh Bachchan, often referred to as the "Shahenshah of Bollywood." His career had many ups and downs. In the early 2000s, he faced significant financial struggles, even being on the brink of bankruptcy. Yet, he didn't give up. Despite the setbacks, he maintained his disciplined work ethic. Bachchan woke up early each day, prepared thoroughly for his roles, and stayed committed to his craft. His comeback as the host of *Kaun Banega Crorepati* reignited his career and helped him repay his debts. Today, his success is not just attributed to his talent but to the discipline and persistence he displayed during challenging times. His story is a testament to the compounding effect of consistent efforts.

Another inspiring story is that of PV Sindhu, the first Indian woman to win a silver medal in badminton at the Olympics. From a young age, she adhered to a strict routine that included waking up at 4 a.m. for training sessions. Her dedication, even in the face of tough training schedules and sacrifices, is what transformed her into a world-class athlete. The discipline she showed by committing to her routine, her diet, and her training paid off, making her a global badminton star. Sindhu's success highlights that discipline in small, everyday actions can create champions.

Virat Kohli is another example of how discipline can lead to remarkable transformation. Early in his career, Kohli was known for his talent but also faced criticism for his fitness. Determined to improve, he adopted a strict fitness regimen and disciplined diet. He worked hard on his endurance and strength, transforming himself into one of the fittest players in the sport. This discipline not only changed his performance but also helped him become one of the most successful captains and players in cricket history. Kohli's story reminds us that the discipline to improve daily habits can lead to profound changes in both health and career.

Then there is Priyanka Chopra Jonas, whose journey from a small town in India to global stardom in Hollywood was marked by consistent dedication. Chopra faced many hurdles as she tried to establish herself internationally, but she stuck to a disciplined routine of honing her acting, singing, and dancing skills. Even today, she is known for her structured daily routine and commitment to her goals, whether in fitness, acting, or entrepreneurship. Chopra's success story emphasizes how disciplined habits can help in breaking barriers and achieving dreams, no matter how big they are.

These success stories show us that discipline is not only about hard work but about creating routines and habits that bring us closer to our goals each day. Each small, disciplined action we take can lead to significant achievements over time. Whether it's sticking to a workout, spending a few minutes each day on a skill, or setting aside time to work on personal goals, these consistent efforts compound into lasting success.

So, take inspiration from these incredible personalities. Start with small, achievable actions today, and let them grow over time.

Discipline is a journey, but the results are worth every step.

Compounding Impact on the Environment

Every action we take has the potential to create a ripple effect. Just like a small stone thrown into a pond creates waves, our choices can lead to bigger changes. This is especially true when it comes to our environment. By making small changes in our daily lives, we can contribute to a healthier planet. These changes may seem minor on their own, but when combined with the actions of others, they can lead to significant improvements.

Sustainable living is about making choices that do not harm our planet. This can be as simple as using reusable bags instead of plastic ones, turning off lights when we leave a room, or using public transport instead of driving.

When many people start doing these small things, it adds up.

Jane Goodall, a famous primatologist and environmental activist, began her career studying chimpanzees in Africa, but over time, her passion for animals led her to advocate for the environment as a whole. Goodall realized that individual actions matter. She founded the Jane Goodall Institute, which focuses on wildlife conservation and the protection of the environment. Her work inspires countless people to take small steps towards sustainability, showing how individual actions can lead to a larger impact.

How Collective Compounding Efforts Can Change the Planet

The power of compounding is not limited to money. It applies to our actions, too. When people come together to make positive changes, the impact can be enormous. Think about recycling. When you recycle a plastic bottle, you help reduce waste. If thousands of people do the same, we can significantly decrease the amount of plastic in landfills and oceans.

This idea of collective action is crucial for tackling environmental issues. When individuals, communities, and organizations join forces, they can create a compounding effect that transforms our planet. For example, the Ocean Conservancy organizes annual beach cleanups worldwide. These events encourage people to come together to clean up our coastlines. As more people participate, the message spreads, inspiring even more individuals to get involved. This collective effort not only cleans our beaches but also raises awareness about the importance of keeping our oceans clean.

Examples of Green Initiatives and Their Ripple Effect

There are many examples of successful green initiatives that showcase the power of compounding. One notable example is Earth Hour, a global event organized by the World Wildlife Fund (WWF). During Earth Hour, millions of people turn off their lights for one hour to raise awareness about climate change. What began as a small initiative in Sydney in 2007 has grown into a worldwide movement. Each year, more cities and individuals participate, showing that small actions can create a significant impact.

TreePeople, an organization based in Los Angeles, dedicated to planting trees and educating communities about the importance of trees for our environment. When TreePeople started, they focused on planting trees in local neighborhoods. Over time, their efforts have led to thousands of trees being planted, improving air quality and providing shade in urban areas. Their work demonstrates how individual efforts can lead to a collective benefit for the community and the environment.

Practical Ways to Start Your Own Compounding Effect for the Environment

Starting your journey toward a more sustainable lifestyle can be simple. Here are some practical ways you can create your own compounding effect for the environment:

1. **Reduce, Reuse, Recycle**

These three R's are the foundation of sustainable living. Reducing waste means buying only what you need. Reusing items can give them a new life. For instance, instead of buying new containers, use jars or boxes you already have at home. Recycling means turning waste into new products, which conserves resources.

2. **Choose Sustainable Products**

When shopping, look for products that are eco-friendly. Choose items made from sustainable materials, like bamboo or recycled plastic. Supporting companies that prioritize the environment encourages more businesses to follow suit. Your choices can lead to a greater demand for sustainable options.

3. Conserve Energy and Water

Simple habits can make a big difference. Turn off lights when you leave a room, use energy-efficient appliances, and take shorter showers. These actions reduce energy and water consumption, helping to conserve our planet's resources.

4. Educate Others

Share what you learn about sustainability with friends and family. When you discuss the importance of protecting our environment, you inspire others to make changes in their lives. The more people who are aware, the greater the impact we can collectively make.

5. **Support Local Initiatives**

Get involved in local environmental initiatives or community gardens. These efforts often rely on volunteers and support from the community. By participating, you not only contribute to your local area but also inspire others to take action.

6. **Plant Trees**

Planting trees is one of the most effective ways to help the environment. Trees absorb carbon dioxide, provide oxygen, and offer habitats for wildlife. You can participate in local tree-planting events or even start your own. Encourage your friends and family to join, and soon you'll create a group dedicated to improving your local environment.

7. Practice Mindful Consumption

Be conscious of what you buy and how it affects the environment. Opt for products with minimal packaging and choose items made from sustainable materials. Mindful consumption reduces waste and encourages companies to produce eco-friendly products.

8. Advocate for Change

Use your voice to advocate for environmental policies that promote sustainability. Write to your local representatives or participate in community meetings to discuss environmental issues. Collective advocacy can lead to significant changes at the local and national levels.

The power of compounding applies to our efforts to protect the environment. Small actions taken by individuals can create a larger impact when combined with the efforts of others. By making simple changes in our lives and encouraging others to do the same, we can create a more sustainable world.

Let us start today, knowing that our collective efforts can lead to meaningful change for the environment. Together, we can create a ripple effect that transforms the world for generations to come.

Challenges to Compounding and How to Overcome Them

Compounding is a powerful concept that can help us grow our skills, knowledge, and even our finances over time. However, like any worthwhile journey, it comes with its own set of challenges. In this chapter, we will discuss some of these challenges and provide simple strategies to overcome them.

The Initial Hardships of Building a Compounding Habit

Starting a new habit can feel like an uphill battle. Imagine trying to push a heavy boulder up a hill. At first, it requires a lot of effort, and progress seems slow. This initial hardship can discourage many people from continuing.

How can you build your compounding habit even when things get tough? One effective strategy is to set small, achievable goals. Instead of focusing on the end result, concentrate on what you can do today. If you want to improve your writing skills, aim to write just one page or even a few sentences each day. Over time, these small efforts will add up, and you'll start to see progress.

Stagnation and Plateaus: Staying Motivated

After some time, you might hit a plateau. This is when you feel like you're putting in the effort, but you're not seeing any results. It can be frustrating and make you wonder if it's even worth continuing. Many people give up during this phase, but there are ways to stay motivated.

Thomas Edison, the inventor of the lightbulb, faced many failures before finally creating a working version. Edison famously said, "I have not failed. I've just found 10,000 ways that won't work." This mindset helped him stay focused even when progress seemed impossible.

To avoid stagnation, try mixing up your routine. If you are learning a new skill, explore different methods or resources. If you're learning to play a musical instrument, switch songs or styles to keep things interesting. Engaging with a community of learners can also provide fresh ideas and encouragement.

Dealing with Criticism and Naysayers

One of the hardest challenges in any journey is dealing with criticism. Whether it comes from friends, family, or even strangers, negative comments can be discouraging. People may not understand your goals or may be skeptical about your ability to achieve them.

When you face criticism, remember that it's often more about the person giving it than about you. You can choose to listen to constructive feedback, which can help you improve, and ignore negative comments that don't serve your goals. Surround yourself with supportive people who encourage your growth. Their positivity can help drown out the negativity and keep you focused on your journey.

How to Recommit When You Lose Momentum

Life is full of ups and downs. Sometimes, we get busy or distracted, and our habits start to slip. It can be easy to feel overwhelmed and think that we will never get back on track. However, recommitting to your goals is possible and can be a rewarding experience.

Michael Jordan, one of the greatest basketball players of all time, faced setbacks, including being cut from his high school basketball team. Instead of giving up, he recommitted to his passion. He practiced relentlessly and eventually became a star player. Jordan's journey teaches us that setbacks are just part of the process.

To regain your momentum, reflect on why you started in the first place. Write down your reasons and revisit them whenever you feel lost. Create a simple action plan that includes small, manageable steps to get back on track. For example, if you want to get back into reading, set a goal to read just a few pages each day. Gradually increase the amount as you regain your habit.

Another helpful strategy is to celebrate your progress, no matter how small. Recognizing your achievements can boost your confidence and motivate you to keep going. For instance, if you've written consistently for a week, reward yourself with something enjoyable, like a favorite snack or a short break to do something you love.

Finally, compounding is a powerful process that can lead to significant growth and achievement over time. However, challenges are a natural part of this journey. By understanding the initial hardships, dealing with stagnation and criticism, and finding ways to recommit when you lose momentum, you can overcome these obstacles.

Everyone faces challenges along the way. The key is to stay focused on your goals, take small steps, and surround yourself with supportive people. Like others, you have the potential to achieve greatness through perseverance and dedication. Keep pushing forward, and the rewards of compounding will come.

The Journey vs. The Destination

In life, we often focus on the destination—where we want to go or what we want to achieve. This is important, but it can sometimes make us overlook the value of the journey itself. The way we get to our goals is just as important, if not more so, than the goals we set for ourselves. Understanding this can help us appreciate the compounding process, which teaches us to value patience, persistence, and the joy of making slow and steady progress.

Why the Path Matters as Much as the Goal

Imagine you are climbing a mountain. The view from the top is breathtaking, but the climb can be tough. Each step you take is part of your adventure, filled with challenges and discoveries. You might meet other climbers, encounter unexpected weather, or find a beautiful spot to rest and enjoy the scenery. All these experiences shape your journey and teach you valuable lessons.

The same is true in life. When we set a goal, we often think only about achieving it. But the steps we take to get there—how we learn, grow, and face challenges—are what truly matter. For example, Thomas Edison, the inventor of the light bulb, faced many failures before he succeeded. He didn't just focus on inventing; he learned from every mistake and kept trying. Each attempt brought him closer to his goal and taught him something new. His journey, filled with trial and error, was as significant as the light bulb itself.

How Compounding Teaches Patience and Perseverance

Compounding is a concept often discussed in finance, but it applies to many areas of life. It means that small actions can build on each other over time, leading to significant results. Think of it like planting a tree. At first, it is just a tiny seed in the ground. You water it, give it sunlight, and wait. It takes time to grow, but eventually, it becomes a strong tree that provides shade and fruit.

In our lives, patience is key. We might want quick results, but real progress often takes time.

The Joy of Slow and Steady Progress

Slow and steady progress can be incredibly fulfilling. It allows us to savor each step along the way and appreciate how far we have come. Each small victory, whether it's learning a new skill, improving our health, or building a relationship, adds up over time. These moments become part of our story.

Olympic athlete, Usain Bolt didn't become a champion overnight. He spent years training, facing setbacks, and improving his technique. Every race, every training session, and even every failure taught him something new. By focusing on his journey and making gradual improvements, he eventually became the fastest man in the world. The joy he felt in those moments of progress was just as important as crossing the finish line first.

Stories of Fulfillment in the Journey

Steve Jobs, co-founder of Apple faced numerous challenges, including being fired from the company he helped create. Instead of giving up, he used that time to reflect and grow. He explored new ideas and eventually returned to Apple, leading it to become one of the most valuable companies in the world. His experiences shaped him into a visionary leader. Jobs taught us that setbacks can be stepping stones to success if we stay committed to our journey.

It's essential to recognize the importance of our journey. Each step we take, each lesson we learn, and each challenge we face contributes to who we are. The process of compounding teaches us that success is not just about reaching the finish line but about the experiences we gain along the way.

By focusing on the journey rather than just the destination, we can develop patience, perseverance, and a deeper appreciation for our progress. Whether we are climbing mountains, writing stories, or pursuing our dreams, let us remember that every moment is part of our unique journey. In the end, the real success lies in how we grow and learn along the way. So, let's cherish the journey and find joy in the compounding process of our lives.

Conclusion

Compounding is a powerful idea. It shows us that small actions can lead to great results over time. This is true in every part of our lives—whether it's in our finances, health, relationships, or personal growth. In this conclusion, we will look at practical steps to get started with compounding in different areas of life, how to overcome doubts, and the vast potential that comes with sticking to your goals.

Practical Steps to Begin Compounding in Each Area of Life

Financial Growth

To start compounding your finances, you don't need a lot of money. Begin by saving a small amount regularly. It could be just a few dollars each week. Over time, this small amount will grow as you earn interest. You can also invest in a savings account or stock market. The key is consistency. Set up an automatic transfer from your checking account to your savings account. This way, you won't forget to save.

Health and Fitness

When it comes to health, start small. If you want to get fit, begin with just 10 minutes of exercise each day. It could be a brisk walk or a few simple stretches. As you get used to this routine, you can gradually increase the time or intensity. Over weeks and months, these small efforts will add up. You will find yourself feeling stronger and healthier without the overwhelming pressure to make drastic changes all at once.

Relationships

Building strong relationships takes time and effort. Start by reaching out to a friend or family member. Send a simple message or make a quick phone call. This small action can help you stay connected. Make it a habit to check in with your loved ones regularly. Over time, these small interactions will strengthen your bonds and create lasting relationships.

Personal Development

If you want to grow personally, begin with reading just a few pages of a book each day. This can be any book that interests you, whether it's fiction or non-fiction. In a month, you will have read several chapters, and in a year, you could finish multiple books. This is how knowledge builds up over time. You can also set small goals, like learning a new word every day.

Career Advancement

In your career, start small by learning one new skill at a time. It could be as simple as taking an online course or watching educational videos. Apply what you learn in your work. As you gain knowledge and experience, you will see the compounding effect in your career, leading to promotions and new opportunities.

Overcoming Doubts and Staying Committed

Doubts can creep in when we try to make changes in our lives. You may think, "Will this really work?" or "I don't have time for this." It's important to remind yourself that everyone starts somewhere. Even the most successful people faced challenges and doubts along their journey.

Staying committed is easier when you remind yourself of your goals. Write them down and keep them visible. Share your goals with friends or family who can support you. This accountability can motivate you to stay on course. Celebrate your small victories along the way. Every little step counts, and acknowledging them can boost your confidence.

The Endless Potential of Compounded Efforts

The beauty of compounding is that its potential is limitless. The more you apply this principle in different areas of your life, the more you will see growth. It's like planting seeds in a garden. At first, you may not see much happening, but with care and patience, those seeds will bloom into beautiful flowers or fruitful plants.

Compounding isn't just about money; it's about progress in every aspect of life. Whether it's skills, knowledge, or health, the cumulative effect of your efforts will lead to amazing outcomes. It might take time, but the journey is worth it.

Final Words of Encouragement on Your Journey

As you begin your journey of compounding, remember that starting small is perfectly fine. The important thing is to take that first step. You don't need to have everything figured out at once. Allow yourself to grow and learn along the way.

When you face obstacles or feel discouraged, think about the bigger picture. The changes you make today will lead to a brighter future. Keep going, even when it feels tough. Surround yourself with positive influences and people who encourage you.

In conclusion, compounding is not just a financial concept; it's a way of life. With every small effort you put in, you are building a foundation for future success. Stay committed, stay positive, and remember that great things take time.

Your journey may be long, but it will be rewarding. Start small, stay the course, and watch as your efforts compound into something extraordinary. You have the power to shape your life, one small step at a time.

Keep moving forward, and you will be amazed at what you can achieve!

<u>Join My Community</u>

https://community.askpndas.com/

www.ingramcontent.com/pod-product-compliance
Lightning Source LLC
Chambersburg PA
CBHW071032240526
45469CB00006BD/2177